Dentists

By Jacqueline Laks Gorman

 **Gareth Stevens** Publishing

Please visit our Web site, www.garethstevens.com. For a free color catalog of all our high-quality books, call toll free 1-800-542-2595 or fax 1-877-542-2596.

Library of Congress Cataloging-in-Publication Data

Gorman, Jacqueline Laks, 1955-
  Dentists / Jacqueline Laks Gorman.
    p. cm. – (People in my community)
  Includes index.
  ISBN 978-1-4339-3801-6 (pbk.)
  ISBN 978-1-4339-3802-3 (6-pack)
  ISBN 978-1-4339-3800-9 (library binding)
  1. Dentists–Juvenile literature. 2. Dentistry–Juvenile literature. 3. Children–Preparation for dental care–Juvenile literature. I. Title.
  RK63.G672 2011
  617.6–dc22
                              2010013205

New edition published 2011 by
Gareth Stevens Publishing
111 East 14th Street, Suite 349
New York, NY 10003

New text and images this edition copyright © 2011 Gareth Stevens Publishing

Original edition published 2003 by Weekly Reader® Books
An imprint of Gareth Stevens Publishing
Original edition text and images copyright © 2003 Gareth Stevens Publishing

Art direction: Haley Harasymiw, Tammy Gruenwald
Page layout: Daniel Hosek, Katherine A. Goedheer
Editorial direction: Kerri O'Donnell, Diane Laska Swanke

Photo credits: Cover, back cover, p. 1 Ron Levine/Photodisc/Getty Images; p. 5 Miguel Alvarez/AFP/ Getty Images; p. 7 © iStockphoto.com; pp. 9, 15, 17, 21 Shutterstock.com; p. 11 Sean Gallup/Getty Images; pp. 13, 19 © Gregg Andersen.

Printed in the United States of America

CPSIA compliance information: Batch #CS10GS: For further information contact Gareth Stevens, New York, New York at 1-800-542-2595.

Table of Contents

Boldface words appear in the glossary.

A Dentist's Job

Do you know what a dentist does? A dentist has an important job. A dentist takes care of people's teeth and mouths.

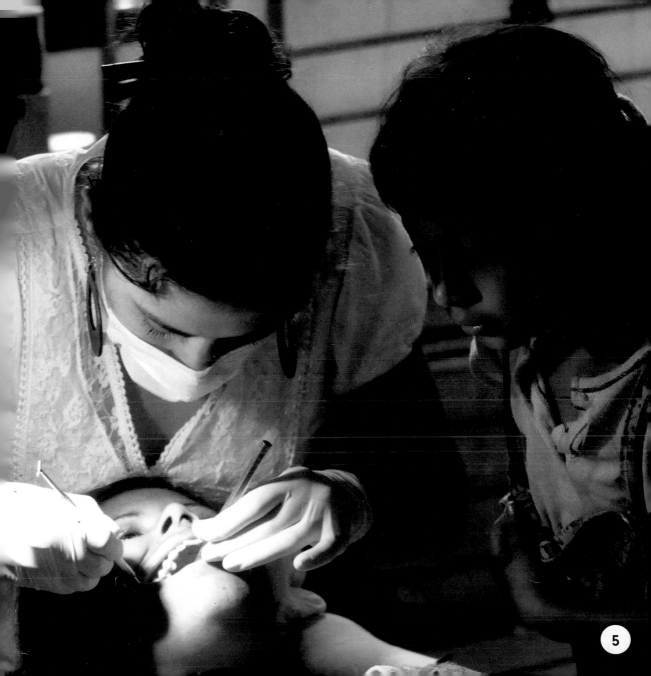

A dentist checks your teeth for **cavities**. A dentist cleans your teeth. He keeps them healthy.

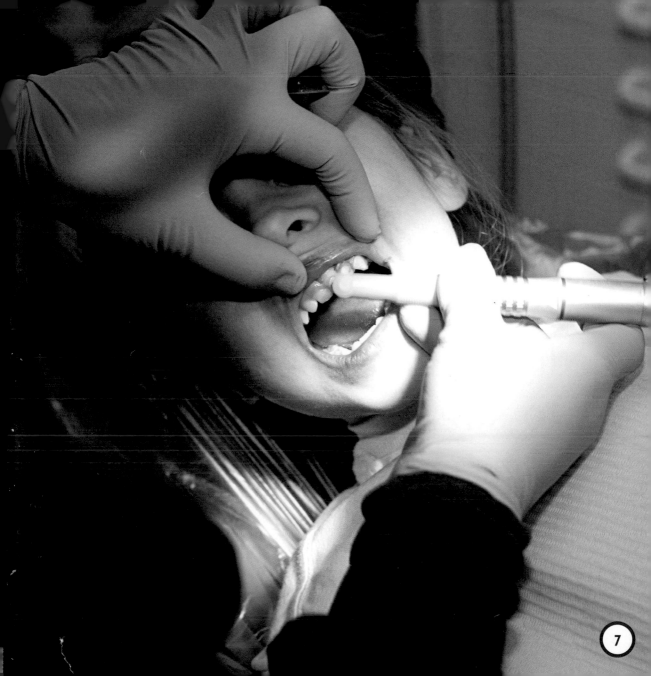

A Dentist's Tools

A dentist has a bright light. She uses the light to see the inside of your mouth.

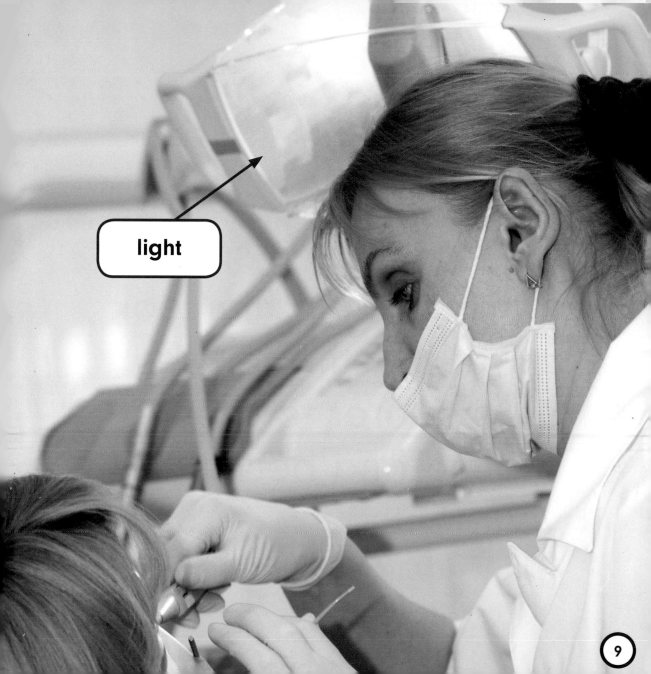

light

A dentist uses special tools. He has a small **mirror** to help him look at your teeth. He uses an **explorer** to check around and between your teeth.

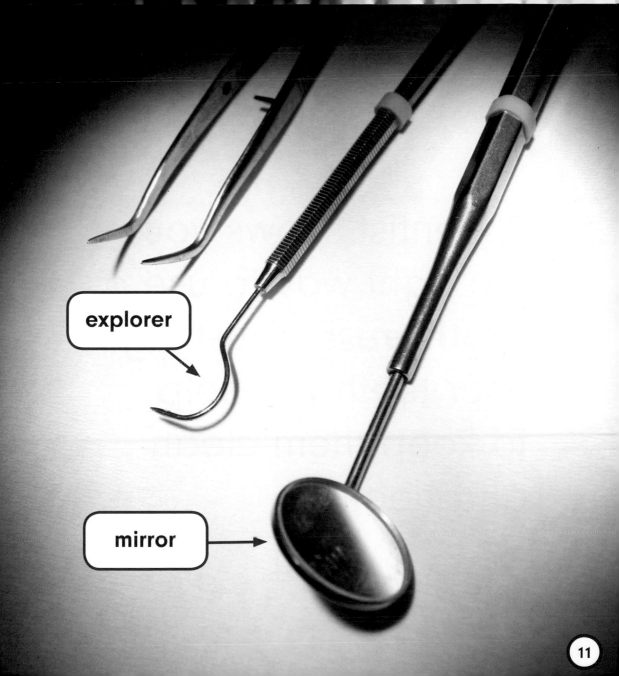

A dentist shows you the right way to use a **toothbrush**. Brushing your teeth will help to keep them clean and healthy.

A dentist may use a special machine to take pictures of your teeth. These pictures are called **X-rays**.

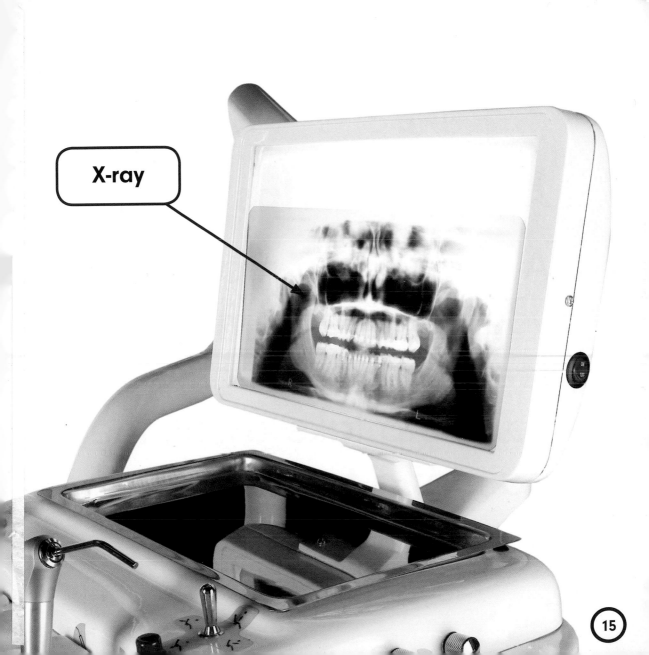

X-ray

A Dentist Helps

A dentist can make your teeth and mouth feel better. A dentist can help take away the pain of a **toothache**.

Going to the dentist will help keep your teeth healthy. You should visit the dentist two times a year.

Would you like to help people keep their teeth and mouths healthy? Would you like to be a dentist?

Glossary

cavities: bad parts of teeth

explorer: a tool that dentists use to check and clean your teeth

mirror: a tool with a shiny side that can show a likeness of something

toothache: a pain in a tooth

toothbrush: a tool used to clean teeth

X-ray: a picture of the inside of something that is taken by a special machine

For More Information

Books

Smith, Penny. *A Trip to the Dentist*. New York, NY: DK Children, 2006.

Ziefert, Harriet. *ABC Dentist: Healthy Teeth from A to Z*. Melbourne, FL: Blue Apple Books, 2008.

Web Sites

American Dental Association: Games & Puzzles
www.ada.org/public/games/games.asp
Enjoy fun games and puzzles as you learn about taking care of your teeth.

Dental Health Month
www.dltk-kids.com/crafts/miscellaneous/dental_health_month.htm
Read poems and stories about healthy teeth. Try coloring and craft projects, too.

Publisher's note to educators and parents: Our editors have carefully reviewed these Web sites to ensure that they are suitable for students. Many Web sites change frequently, however, and we cannot guarantee that a site's future contents will continue to meet our high standards of quality and educational value. Be advised that students should be closely supervised whenever they access the Internet.

Index

About the Author

Jacqueline Laks Gorman is a writer and editor. She grew up in New York City and began her career working on encyclopedias and other reference books. Since then, she has worked on many different kinds of books. She lives with her husband and children, Colin and Caitlin, in DeKalb, Illinois.